IS
in the Mirror

Life Stories of a Jewish Girl Raised in the 50s

DEBI NEVEL DRECKSLER

Travel is Life
P.O. Box 25014
Asheville NC 28813-0014
www.travelislife.org

Copyright © 2022 by Debi Nevel Drecksler

All rights reserved. This book or any portion thereof may not be reproduced or used in any manner whatsoever without the express written permission of the publisher except for the use of brief quotations in a book review. The information in this book is true and complete to the best of our knowledge. All recommendations are made without any guarantee on the part of the author or publisher, who also disclaim any liability incurred in connection with the use of this data or specific details.

Printed in the United States of America

First Edition 2022

ISBN: 978-0-9977710-3-9

A big thank you to the following people and groups for their help and encouragement in bringing this book to life!

To my husband, Richard Drecksler. For the countless times I asked you, "May I please read you just one more story?" You listened, critiqued my work and most importantly, loved me through this entire process.

To my son, Paul Drecksler. There are not enough words to describe how much I appreciate all the long hours and hard work you put into preparing my book for publication. You are an amazingly talented man and I adore you.

To my friend and gifted artist, Mayra Mogavero. You created cover artwork that was exactly what I imagined. I am forever grateful to you.

To my friend Bracha Betty Jacob. Thank you for helping me check my Yiddish throughout the book.

To the Facebook group, *Yiddish Word of the Day*. You have become my extended family. So many of you have supported my dream to publish a book of my short stories. Your loving words have stayed in my heart.

To the Facebook group, *Children of Exile-A Cuban Diary*. Several years ago you made me an honorary member and encouraged me to share my stories. So many of you have become my friends.

To my friend and talented author, Linda Lou. Thank you for inspiring and motivating me to write this book.

Table of Contents

CHILDHOOD

The Gift of Life 14
The Sleepover 16
Sundays at the Park 18
Fun in the 50s 20
The Assortment of Children 21
Losing Bubbi 23
My Exceptional Role Models 25
The Temple Show 27
My Father The Healer 29
Proud To Be Their Daughter 31
A Mother's Day Story 33
Hurricane Donna 35
Cherished Memories 37
My Mother, My Hero 39
An Angel on Earth 41
The File Cabinet 43
A Father's Love 45
A Gift From My Father 47
The Love Goddess 49
A Precious Memory 51
The Tin Box 53
The Crush 56
Building Bridges Not Barriers 58
Value People More Than Things 60
Zaydie Nevelsky 62

EARLY ADULT YEARS

Soulmates 66
Do You Believe In Bashert 68
Richard and Debi's Wedding 70
The Birth of My First Child 72
A Special Friendship 74
Yes Darling,...She Got It From You 77
My Mother's Forever Love 79
Such a Love 81
I Would Not Be Invisible 83
The Poetry Book 85
My Father's Daughter 87
The Clock 89
Wolfie's 21 Girl 92
Love Makes A Home 94
Mommy Has Gone To Heaven 96
The Birthday Gift 98
The Phone Call I Will Never Forget 100
I Can't Stay Silent Anymore 103
Between Two Friends 105
I'm Married To A Movie Star 108
My 30 Seconds Of Fame 110
The Very Special Anniversary 112
The Dancer 114
Kindness of a Stranger 117
The Tape 119

FAMILY & FRIENDS

How Bubbi & Zaydie Met 122
My Father's Passion For Yiddish 124
A Letter To My Aunt Elizabeth 126

Spunky Aunt Annie 128
Unconditional Love 130
The Road Trip 132
The Neighbor 134
The Nevelsky Brothers 136
Look For The Good 138
The Cooking Pot 140
Aunt Shirley 143
Aunt Betty's Mitzvah 145
A Special Cousin 147
The Penny Jar 149
Worthy of Love 151
My Angel 153
My Father-in-Law 155
A Letter To My Brother 157
Remembering Bubbi 159

MODERN DAY

The Momma 162
The Love Notes 164
The Jewish Mother 166
My Three Gifts Next Door 168
Crumbled Cakes & All 170
Bonus Family 171
The Dream 173
The Little Things 175
The Storyteller 177

Intro

In the 1950s, there was nothing I loved more than sitting with my Father and listening to stories about our family. His expressive voice would make every story magical.

As a child, I developed close relationships with my extended family. For me, it was an opportunity to learn more about them and create new memories.

Writing stories allows me to recapture moments that impacted my life and share my family history.

I hope when you read my stories you are transported back to your own special times.

Enjoy the trip down memory lane.

~ Debi Nevel Drecksler

*Names have been changed in some stories.

About The Author

Debi Nevel Drecksler was born in South Florida. She attended college in Atlanta where she received her B.A. in Education. In 1973, after teaching school in Atlanta, she moved back to South Florida. In 1987, she and her family moved to North Carolina where she currently resides.

Debi has worked as a teacher, recreation director, newspaper and magazine columnist, and radio show host. She has owned and operated two businesses.

Writing is her passion, and her human interest stories have entertained readers for years.

Debi lives with her husband, Richard, in Candler, N.C. They are the parents of four children and have several grandchildren.

CHILDHOOD

The Gift of Life

When my Mother was in labor with me at Mercy Hospital in Miami, Florida, her Doctor was nowhere to be found. The staff attempted to stop my Mother from giving birth until the Doctor arrived. My Father could hear his wife's screams from down the hall.

The Doctor finally showed up, and my Mother birthed her nine pound baby girl. I was placed in a bassinet and brought to the nursery.

Shortly after I was born, a Nun / Nurse was walking past my bassinet and leaned down to get a good look at the newest baby in the nursery. She was horrified to see that I had turned purple and was not breathing. My lungs had collapsed from the traumatic birth.

Screaming for help, she and a medical team brought me back to life!

My Mother shared this story with me when I was old enough to understand. I know she wanted me to appreciate how blessed I was to be alive and healthy.

I wish I could go back and thank the Nun at Mercy Hospital for saving the life of a Jewish baby, whose parents named her Devora Rivka.

I've always believed she was my Angel.

Ikh lbn yeder tag dankbar tsu zeyn lebedik.

(I live every day grateful to be alive.)

The Sleepover

When I was a little girl, I begged my parents to let me sleep over my Bubbi and Zaydie's apartment. They finally consented.

That night Bubbi made a delicious chicken dinner in her big pot. She and Zaydie conversed in Yiddish as I gobbled up my food. She cooked differently than my Mother (more old country), and I loved it.

After dinner, we sat in their comfy living room until I grew very tired. Bubbi tucked me into their bed. I would be sleeping in the middle of the two of them.

Hours later, I woke up abruptly and started to scream. There was enough light in their bedroom to see two drinking glasses, one on each nightstand. In the glasses were teeth soaking in a liquid.

Both my grandparents woke up and tried to calm me down. I stared in horror at two toothless people who looked like strangers to me.

"Where are my Bubbi and Zaydie?" I cried. "What have you done with them?"

My Bubbi got up and ran to the phone in the kitchen. I could hear her talking to my Father in Yiddish.

Thirty minutes later, my Father came to take me home. He gave his parents big hugs, and they chatted a few minutes in Yiddish. On the ride home, he told me that no one was upset with me.

I have never forgotten that night!

Sundays at the Park

In the 1950s, Sundays were often spent at a park where Bubbi, Zaydie, four of the Nevelsky siblings (who lived in South Florida) and their children would gather to spend time together.

The grownups would sit in the shade talking away in Yiddish with the exception of a few of the siblings' spouses, who though Jewish, did not speak Yiddish fluently. They would converse with each other.

The cousins always had fun chasing each other around the park, laughing and teasing each other.

I remember one time Bubbi walking up to my cousin, Leon, who was the closest in age to me, and telling him to give me a kiss.

Leon scrunched up his nose and said, "YUCK! She's a girl. I would never kiss a girl!"

Decades later, I flew down to South Florida for a family member's wedding and saw Leon sitting alone at a table watching everyone dance. He looked exactly like that six year old boy, except he was very tall and had long hair.

I walked up to him and his face lit up. We chatted, and I reminded him of that incident from when we were children.

He looked up at me and grinned. In a very deep voice he said, "I certainly wouldn't turn you down now!"

*In blessed memory of my beloved cousin Leon who took the stairway to heaven.

Fun in the 50s

In the 50s, my main transportation was a pair of roller skates. Living in Coral Gables, Florida with lots of sidewalks and no fear of being snatched by predators back then, my brother and I would skate our way around the neighborhood, waving at neighbors and occasionally being chased by friendly dogs.

As the steaming hot South Florida sun peaked at noon, we would make our way home, knowing that a freshly squeezed glass of orange juice and a peanut butter and jelly sandwich would be waiting for us. Then back outside to skate some more!!

At night, I'd crawl into bed SO tired, drifting off to sleep on crisp sheets, dried on a clothesline and scented by the sun.

It was a wonderful time to be a child.

Aza a gliklekh zkrun!

(Such a happy memory!)

The Assortment of Children

My Mother had a terrific sense of humor which served her well.

My older brother and I were only 21 months apart in age. My Mother didn't drive and would take us out daily for long walks in our double stroller. People would smile at the little blond haired boy with green eyes and the little girl with curly red hair and brown eyes.

They would often ask my Mother, a tall dark haired beauty, "Are you the Nanny?"

She would laugh and reply, "Why yes, I guess I am!"

What she didn't add was she was also the housekeeper, laundress and cook.

She eventually went on to have three more children. Together we were two redheads, two shades of blonde and one brunette, all of us from the same parents.

Once, a woman questioned my Mother about birthing an "assortment" of children who didn't look anything like her.

Without missing a beat, my adorable Mother replied, "Maybe my husband fooled around?"

The confused look on the *yenta's* (busybody) face was priceless!

Losing Bubbi

I woke up on September 28th, 1958 to a houseful of people. I was seven years old and SO excited that this many people would show up to celebrate my little sister's third birthday.

Sadly, that wasn't why.

My twin Aunties, my Mother's sisters, sat me down to talk to me. They explained that my beloved Bubbi had died during the night. She had been living with us for a few weeks and though mostly bedridden, always had a sweet smile on her face.

As a little girl, I just assumed Bubbi was very tired and needed to rest. I would watch my Father go in and talk to her for hours, always in Yiddish, his Mother's fragile hand gently wrapped in his big, strong one. I would watch from the bedroom door and just feel the love.

The memories are as clear as day. I had a difficult time understanding there would be no more Bubbi, who smelled like chicken soup, was always happy and had the softest skin. I knew my Father adored his Mother, and at thirty seven years old, with four children and another on the way, wasn't ready to say goodbye

It was the first time I saw my Father cry.

My Exceptional Role Models

In the mid-1950s, my parents and other Jewish families participated with their children in a peaceful march for Civil Rights. As we walked along the streets of Miami, there were angry people screaming insults at us.

I was only five years old and quite confused at all the commotion. All we were doing was standing up for the people of color, who, in our city, couldn't drink out of our water fountains, sit with us on buses or attend our schools.

When I would question my Mother about these things, she would always say, "The people who make the rules are not very smart."

My Mother took my hand while we marched and said, "Debi, please stare straight ahead and keep walking. Ignore the people who feel it necessary to be so hateful."

Then she added words that to this day profoundly affected me… "Change doesn't happen if you sit on the sidelines!"

No one harmed us that afternoon. As I look back more than six decades later, I am SO proud of my Mother and Father, the children of immigrants, for standing up for their convictions. Their generation lived through the horrors of the Holocaust, and they wanted to teach their children....

Every man, woman and child deserves to be treated with respect, regardless of their race, religion or ethnic background.

Thank you, dear parents, for being such exceptional role models

The Temple Show

My older brother and I were very close in age, and as little children, were inseparable.

There was a show at our Synagogue that we decided to participate in. We rehearsed our song together a dozen times at home with our Father accompanying us on the piano.

We were SO excited the day of the show. The accompanist had our music and everything was in order.

When our names were called, we came out onto the stage and saw our parents smiling at us from the audience.

As the music began, we realized the pianist was playing it in the wrong key!! It was WAY too high for us. I started to panic!!

Big brother whispered in my ear, "We can do this!!"

Holding hands, we screeched out those high notes and made it through the song!!

"Go down, Moses. Way down in Egypt's Land. Tell ol' Pharaoh... Let my people go!!"

With flushed *punims* (faces) and still clutching hands, we took our bows to the marvelous sounds of applause.

Big brother and I have never forgotten our performance. One of many sweet memories we share.

My Father The Healer

When I was a child, whenever I was sick, my Father would put his hands on my *keppie* (forehead), and within minutes I would feel better. He would sing in Yiddish, and his melodic voice would lull me to sleep.

My Father was a healer, and it was a gift he used wisely. People often commented how much better they felt after spending time with him. A cousin, who was a Doctor, would visit my Father whenever his back pain became unbearable. He would always leave with a smile on his face.

I believe my Father's "gift", along with his genuine love of people, was what kept him going for many years after a Cancer diagnosis. To him, dying wasn't an option.

I wanted to believe my Father would live forever.

Twenty years after his death, people are still telling me the positive impact he had on their lives. It makes me cry happy tears.

If I close my eyes, I can still feel his gentle touch and his warm breath upon my *keppie* as he kisses me goodnight.

Proud To Be Their Daughter

In the late 1950s, after attending kindergarten and first grade at the Hebrew Academy, my parents enrolled me in public school.

I remember the first day my Mother walked me to school. We left the house a little early so I could meet the teacher before my classmates arrived.

As we approached the campus, I noticed a group of black children standing behind a chain link fence staring at us.

I waved at them excitedly and asked my Mother, "I wonder if any of those children will be in my class?"

My Mother answered, "No Debi, they go to a different school."

I gave my Mother a confused look. "They live right next door to the school. Why don't they go to MY school?"

My Mother replied, "That's because the people who make the rules are not very smart."

As a child, I asked a lot of questions, and my parents always took the time to answer them. They never sugarcoated their replies, choosing instead to honestly explain things to me in a way that I could understand.

Both my Father and Mother were raised by Russian immigrant parents, who taught them to respect people of all races, religions and ethnic groups. Their parents believed this strongly, regardless of any discrimination they were subjected to as Jews in the old country or after they emigrated.

This is how my beloved parents raised their own children, too. The five of us had the very best role models.

I am proud to be their daughter.

A Mother's Day Story

It was the late 1950s, and I had saved my allowance (twenty-five cents per week) to buy my Mother something very special for Mother's Day.

One Saturday, I walked to Miracle Mile in Coral Gables accompanied by my big brother / bodyguard. We went into Woolworth's, where my favorite sales lady, Hazel, was more than happy to assist me.

I proudly shared with Hazel that I had $1.00 to spend on a Mother's day gift. She showed me lipsticks and tiny bottles of perfume. Then I saw it -- a pin with my Mother's name on it!! I was excited that even with tax, I could afford it!

Hazel wrapped it up for me in a piece of colored tissue paper, which I was sure she saved for special gifts like this. I thanked her for her help. After stopping at A&P for ice cream cones, a treat from big brother, (ten cents for a double dip) we walked home, and I hid my gift.

On Mother's Day, I presented my Mother with her gift. She gave me a huge hug and attached my pin on her gorgeous, flowy dress. She wore it proudly to her Mother's Day dinner party.

After my Mother died, I discovered it wrapped in the original tissue paper in her jewelry box.

After unwrapping it, I realized that I had given my Mother a name pin for a waitress!!

I couldn't believe she wore it on her gorgeous dress to that elegant Mother's Day dinner!!

I cried thinking how much she loved me.

Hurricane Donna

On September 10th, 1960, Hurricane Donna roared through South Florida causing extensive damage.

I remember the hurricane like it was yesterday. After our Father boarded up the house, we all huddled together in the hot, humid living room, listening to the wind howling and wreaking havoc outside.

The baby was crying, and the children were whining that they were hungry. The power had gone off, so meals consisted of peanut butter & jelly sandwiches and fig newton cookies.

Big brother David could see that our normally mild tempered Father was getting aggravated with our behavior. He called a "secret" meeting where he convinced three of his siblings (the baby was excluded) to put books in their pants.

David's explanation was, "If Daddy goes to *potch* (spank) us, we won't feel a thing!"

We made our way back into the living room with solemn expressions. All of a sudden our Mother starts laughing, but our Father doesn't catch on. She's laughing so hard she can't even talk. All she can do is point to our *tushies*.

Big brother starts laughing next, realizing he is NOT going to get in trouble. Then we all start laughing, including our Father.

It was a catastrophic hurricane, but we survived on love and laughter.

Cherished Memories

When I was a little girl, summer vacations meant a week on Miami Beach. My parents would rent a little place only fifteen miles from where we lived in Coral Gables. We'd spend the week swimming in the ocean and enjoying the beach.

During these years, my Mother was pregnant three times in four years, so it was not unusual to see her relaxing on a beach chair while we played.

My big brother and I would build sand castles while the little ones watched. They would be spectacular (at least through our eyes), and fabulous stories would be created with the two of us the main characters.

We always looked forward to the ice cream truck. You could hear the music so you knew when it was coming. A nickel would buy you a scrumptious treat guaranteed to cool you off on a blistery hot day.

My Mother allowed my big brother and me to go fishing off the pier. She knew the seasoned fishermen would keep an eye on us.

One time we caught a barracuda, and they helped us take it off our hook and throw it back. They laughed at how excited we were!! I wish I had brought my little brownie camera to photograph the moment.

Those were special summers never to be forgotten.

I cherish the memories.

My Mother, My Hero

In 1961, when I was in the 6th grade, my teacher, Mr. Thompson, told the class that the art assignment that day was to make our parents' Christmas cards. I raised my hand and asked the teacher if I could make a Chanukah card for my Father because he was a religious Jew. Mr. Thompson's face turned beet red. He picked up a book from his desk and threw it at me hitting my shoulder.

Needless to say, I never got to make my Chanukah card that day, nor did I make a Christmas card.

When I arrived home from school, I told my Mother what happened. Remaining very calm, she asked me to watch my three younger siblings for a short while. Not knowing how to drive a vehicle, she got on her bicycle and pedaled away.

She went to my classroom, and though the school day was over, my teacher was still there.

My Mother said, "Mr. Thompson... If I EVER hear of you physically or emotionally abusing my child again, I will report you to the American Civil Liberties Union and several other organizations I belong to. My daughter WILL make a Chanukah card tomorrow, which she will bring home to our family. Is that understood?"

Mr. Thompson looked at my Mother with huge eyes, didn't say a word, but nodded his head.

Bracha Barnett Nevel, a 36 year old Mother of five and daughter of Russian / Jewish immigrants, rode home on her bicycle with her head held high.

This antisemitic teacher never disrespected me again.

My beloved Mother was and always will be my HERO.

An Angel on Earth

Faye was one of my Mother's best friends and treated her like a sister. She wasn't able to have children, but loved my siblings and me like family.

When my older brother was preparing for his Bar Mitzvah, Faye planned a special day just for me.

She lived in an adorable little apartment on South Beach, filled with unique items that she had collected through the years. Each keepsake had a story behind it, so you can imagine how interested I was to hear all her stories.

That morning, Faye took me to a fabric shop and had me pick out any material I wanted. She was planning to create a gorgeous dress for me to wear to my brother's party. I chose an emerald green taffeta, which Faye said complemented my auburn hair. After that, we went to a shop filled with colorful costume jewelry, and she bought me an emerald pin to go with my dress.

Faye took me to a gourmet market where she let me choose anything I wanted for lunch. Then we went back to her apartment, where she served the delectable food on her most elegant dishes. After lunch, she "fitted" me for the dress.

A week later, Faye came over with the dress. It was magnificent!!

My brother's Bar Mitzvah was a memorable occasion, and the party afterwards was so much fun. Everyone loved my emerald green dress.

Faye passed away a month after my brother's Bar Mitzvah. I never knew she had cancer. She asked my Mother not to tell me, and my Mother respected her wishes. I was heartbroken.

I've always believed Faye was *mlakh aoyf der erd* (an Angel on earth) who made a little girl feel like a beautiful princess before she joined the other Angels in heaven.

Another blessing in my life.

The File Cabinet

When I was in elementary school, I had a school project that had to be completed by the next day. I was attempting to sketch the flowers and birds of each state and was failing miserably.

My Father came home from work that night and saw the look of frustration on my face. He didn't criticize me for procrastinating, choosing instead to help me get the project done. We stayed up way past my bedtime, and finally it was completed! I was so grateful to my Father for his help.

Decades later, my Father offered me a very heavy duty filing cabinet for my home office. He was downsizing and thought I would appreciate it. My husband and I went to his house to pick it up. He had wrapped it in a blanket to help keep it from getting dented while we transported it.

When we got home and took off the blanket, much to my surprise, on the side of the file cabinet, my Father had taped the extra flowers and birds from the childhood project we had worked on together.

Since then, that file cabinet has traveled with us hundreds of miles to four different homes.

My Father's beautiful artwork will stay taped to the side of that file cabinet forever. It brings me such joy to look at it.

Es meynt alts far mir.

(It means everything to me.)

A Father's Love

When I was a little girl, I had a speech impediment. The school suggested a speech therapist, but my Father said he would like the opportunity to work with me first.

I couldn't pronounce my Rs, and I remember my Father spending hours teaching me how to twirl my tongue and say Roy Rogers over and over again. If I got frustrated, he would never get upset at me, instead encouraging me to keep on practicing.

I finally overcame my speech impediment thanks to my Father's patience and commitment to helping me succeed.

Decades later...

In 2007, I was assaulted one night in a highway rest stop, and my eyes were injured. The Doctors told me the damage was irreversible. I was terrified of going blind and became extremely depressed. I felt hopeless.

One night I had a dream. I was a little girl again, and my Father was having me practice my speech lessons over and over.

He said, "You can do this, Debi! Never give up!!"

Though my Father was in heaven, I knew he was reaching out to me to stay fearless and resilient. Whatever the future held, he was sending me a message that every day was worth living to the fullest.

He was there for me when I needed him.

A Father's love is forever.

*My eyes no longer dilate properly, and I can't see well in natural or artificial light, but I did not go blind. I am so grateful to still have my vision.

A Gift From My Father

My father worked long hours, but he found ways to balance his life by spending time with his large family and finding outlets for his creative energy.

I remember when I was a child, my Father auditioned for a theatrical production. The part required him to wear a toupee. After a rehearsal one night, he walked into the house with a headful of wavy hair. The five children came running when they heard Mother's laughter, and soon everyone was hysterical.

My good natured Father decided to go back and tell the Director that he would prefer to do the part as a *"debonair"* bald man. The Director agreed.

My Father loved painting. Having been raised as an Orthodox Jew, he enjoyed bringing his memories to life. He would put his heart and soul into his artwork. I am proud to have one of his beautiful creations in my home.

His passion was Yiddish. Translating stories, poetry and songs brought him hours of enjoyment. Besides translating for I.B. Singer, he worked with Yiddish poets. He loved the language and spoke it fluently.

I rarely saw my Father sit and watch television, but I would often see him reading. He loved Jewish literature and comedy. He had a marvelous sense of humor.

I always feel my Father's spirit surrounding me. Besides his red hair and freckles, I was blessed with his creative energy. Stories dance in my head, and I love writing them!

Thank you, dear Father, for the gift.

The Love Goddess

When my Mother and her sisters were growing up, college was not an option. I think my Grandpa just assumed they would all get married young and have babies.

My twin Aunties ended up going to college on the GI bill after serving in the Navy, and my Mother enrolled after her five children were old enough to fend for themselves.

I remember my Mother filling out the application.

One of the questions was, "If you are currently not in high school or college and there has been a gap in your education, please tell us in detail what you have been doing."

I saw the look on my Mother's face and knew this was going to be interesting.

Would she write that she's been raising five children for the past twenty years and describe all her domestic duties?

Would she talk about baking cupcakes for PTA meetings?

Of course not!!

My beautiful, spirited Mother wrote, "I've been a love Goddess!"

As I'm sure you can imagine... She had a lot of fun going to college.

A Precious Memory

It was the early 60s and I was living in Coral Gables, Florida.

While skating or riding my bicycle around the neighborhood, I often passed a young couple. They looked to be about sixteen. She had very long golden hair swept up in a ponytail, always adorned with a ribbon. He was strikingly handsome.

This angelic looking girl would be pushing the young man's wheelchair and chattering away. He was always smiling.

One day I saw them coming out of the A&P. She was gently wiping his mouth as he devoured an ice cream cone. It was a sweltering hot day, so the idea of an ice cream cone was very appealing. I greeted them as I headed into the grocery store for my own treat.

I saw them many times over the next few months and always waved. I wanted to stop and talk to them but never knew exactly what to say. I was just a preteen and they were a teenage couple obviously in love.

While their classmates were dancing to the music of Chubby Checker and frolicking at Crandon Park Beach, they were enjoying each other's company along the sidewalks in Coral Gables.

I never forgot this beautiful couple and hope they lived happily ever after.

For me, the recollection is...

A teyerer zkhrun.

(A precious memory.)

The Tin Box

My Zaydie lived alone in a small apartment on South Beach. I would often go visit him, and he would always offer me this brittle candy he made. It was sweet and delicious, but you had to be careful it didn't crack your teeth.

Zaydie and I would sit together and *shmooze*. He would often stop and hold his tummy but never complain. My Father had shared that Zaydie had stomach cancer but had asked me not to reveal I knew. He wanted my visits to be happy and uplifting.

Zaydie's English was limited, so mostly I chatted away. He would just smile and stare at me. My Father told me when I was a little girl, I bore a striking resemblance to my Aunt Evelyn who died of pneumonia in her early 20s.

There I sat with the same red hair and freckles, wondering if Zaydie was seeing his deceased daughter, who like me, was outgoing and conversational. Or was he seeing his granddaughter Debi?

When Zaydie died, family came to his apartment and took his belongings... a TV, radio and a few pieces of furniture. My Father waited patiently until everyone left. Sitting in a corner hardly noticed was a very old but beautifully crafted tin box my Zaydie had made. My Father took it home, happy to have this cherished keepsake.

That evening, we children gathered around as our Father showed us the box Zaydie had created with his own hands. Suddenly a trap door opened up. It was filled with all denomination of bills. Our eyes grew large as our Father counted it. Zaydie, like many of his generation, was most likely saving money for a rainy day.

My Father donated the money to charity in Zaydie's blessed memory.

Decades later, my Father took out the box to show me. It had been covered with paint, which through the years had been peeling away.

I asked if I could please have the box. Without hesitating, he agreed.

I've always believed my Father knew I would be the one to tell its story.

The Crush

When I was fifteen, I had a crush on a brilliant young man with eyes the color of the ocean and a smile that lit up a room. His Mother made the most scrumptious Friday night dinners, which I was often invited to. His family didn't drive on Shabbat, so he would walk over and escort me to his home, several blocks away.

My Mother was always happy to see him and was a charming hostess while I would finish primping. I wanted to look just perfect!!

He went away to college that Fall and wrote me long descriptive letters. He planned to become a Doctor, so most of his time was spent studying.

One day, I was talking to my Mother and she blurts out, "Knowledge is my mistress!"

I stared at her and asked, "Where did you hear that line?"

She replied, "Oh, I was putting away some clean laundry and there was this letter on your dresser. I tried not to read it but couldn't stop myself!"

I wanted to get mad at my Mother but couldn't. She had the most apologetic expression on her face.

"Mom, I would greatly appreciate if you wouldn't read my private mail."

She looked at me and replied, "I'll never do it again! I promise!!"

As my Mother, a lover of poetic verse, walked away, she winked at me and added, "Find a good hiding place."

Building Bridges Not Barriers

Having a big brother came with its benefits. Though fiercely protective, my brother never stood in the way of me enjoying a social life.

One summer day, after boarding at a Yeshiva high school for a year, my brother came home with several of his classmates. He introduced each one to me. I gave them my most engaging smile.

We had just moved from Coral Gables, Florida to Miami Beach, and I was hoping to make some new friends before starting my junior year.

Thanks to big brother, my social calendar was filled every weekend, and I was quickly accepted into their circle of friends.

Those classmates and their families were warm and loving to my brother and me even though we were not being raised as Orthodox Jews.

Our Mother was a Jewish book reviewer for a local newspaper and head librarian at our reform synagogue. Our Father volunteered with Jewish youth groups and conducted services for the Jewish holidays at local nursing homes.

Our parents were *gute mentshn* (good people), and this is what touched people's hearts when they met them, not what synagogue they attended.

Having an opportunity to grow up in that kind of nonjudgmental environment, with a family I loved so much, influenced the person I am today.

My life is about building bridges, not putting up barriers.

I can't imagine living any other way.

Value People More Than Things

When I was in high school, I had a part time job doing office work for my Father's business on South Beach. As I quietly stood in the corner of his office filing large stacks of papers, I would listen to my Father interact with customers. He had such a warm personality, and people really felt comfortable with him.

My Father had a philosophy that worked for the occasional grumpy person who felt it necessary to be loud. It was...

"The louder they yell, the softer YOU speak."

It worked every time!

After many decades, my Father sold his business, and in his later years of life, purchased a restaurant called Wolfie's 21 on Miami Beach. There, he was able to do what he loved best... interact with people from all walks of life while they enjoyed a scrumptious meal.

He met movie stars, musicians, politicians and fascinating people from all over the world.

My Father was the smiling gentleman who'd show up at your table and say, "It is a pleasure to have you dine with us. Which one of our world famous desserts may I interest you in today?"

He would never just say, "Did you leave room for dessert?"

I learned so much from my Father, more than anything I ever read in a textbook.

Most importantly, I learned to...

Value people more than things.

Zaydie Nevelsky

My paternal grandfather, who I called Zaydie, had twenty-five grandchildren. I was one of the oldest and had the joy of spending time with him.

He passed away when I was nineteen.

Zaydie lived in a small apartment on South Beach. When I visited him, he always offered me some hard brittle candy that he made. I had to break it into very small pieces so it wouldn't crack my teeth.

He would join me at the table and have a little schnapps, and as he said, "For medicinal purposes only."

Zaydie spoke mostly Yiddish. Between his shul, his friends and the nearby shops that catered to Jewish clientele, he could converse in Yiddish all day.

One day Zaydie decided to have the "talk" with me. He said that I needed to have a Yiddish line to tell the Jewish boys who wanted to go out with me.

It was, "*Ikh bin a gut meydl.*" ("I am a good girl.")

He had me practice the line until it was memorized.

He told me I was a lovely, intelligent young woman and should never let a man take advantage of me.

I never forgot the Yiddish he taught me or the lesson in self-respect.

EARLY ADULT YEARS

Soulmates

I believe that many of our experiences in life happen exactly as they are supposed to.

When I was in college in Atlanta, I met a Jewish student from New York who swept me off my feet. Having a loving but strict Father, I knew that living together was not even a consideration. We were married six months after our first date. I was twenty years old.

Though the marriage didn't survive, I was blessed with a beautiful, healthy son. I can't imagine life without him.

I've never looked back with regret at my first marriage.

A few months later, I received a call from Richard, a former high school classmate / family friend. He asked me out. I invited him to my apartment for lunch instead. He showed up at my door with a red race car for my son. He leaned down and handed it to him before giving me a hug.

After lunch, he invited me out for dinner the following night. I asked if I could bring my son.

He replied, "Of course. I was expecting him to join us."

I knew right then I would marry this man.

Two years earlier...

Being friends of the family, Richard and his Mother were invited to my son's *Pidyon Haben,* a Jewish ceremony for first born sons that involves the transfer of five silver coins. At the time, I was still married to my first husband. My Father had forgotten the silver coins, but by some stroke of luck, someone had thought to bring five silver coins and handed them to my Father. It was Richard!!

Another interesting fact... My baby was born on Richard's Grandmother's birthday.

As the Rabbi said at our wedding, Richard and I were true soulmates.

Do You Believe In Bashert

One evening in 1976, my brother, who was living in South Florida, was eating dinner with a group of friends.

Not being shy, David hollers across the table to one of the fellows, "My sister is back in town. You should give her a call."

That young man he singled out remembers David's sister from high school. They sat next to each other in homeroom and were always friendly to each other. His widowed Mother and her parents socialized together at the synagogue.

Eight years later, here was big brother, known for being very protective of his little sister, giving his blessing.

Through the years, my older brother and I have talked about this. Was it *bashert* (destiny) that both my brother and my husband (yes, I married this wonderful man) were eating dinner together with a group of friends on that exact night?

What if either of them had decided at the last minute to stay home?

Would I be married to my soulmate for over forty-five years?

Richard and Debi's Wedding

I do not have one single photograph of my wedding. Both photographers, one a family member and the other a friend, claim their cameras malfunctioned.

Some might think that this is quite sad, but my memories are vivid. With words, I can create a visual of that special day in my life.

Jan 16th, 1977

I take one final look in the mirror, adjusting my flowered headband that complements my flowy blue dress, before taking my son's hand. Richard, dressed in a navy suit, takes his other hand, and together the three of us head toward the chapel.

A well-meaning friend tries to convince me to let my little boy to go sit with his grandparents. I politely decline. He wants to be in the ceremony. He is part of this new beginning.

The Rabbi smiles as we walk toward him. Both our families have belonged to his synagogue for years. He tells us performing this ceremony brings him such *nachas* (joy).

My Father stands up and makes a toast at the party, accidentally referring to his new Son-in-law by my ex-husband's name. The room becomes very silent. Richard walks up and kisses his new Father-in-law's cheek. This seals their friendship for life. *L'chayim!!* (To life!!)

The next day at Disney World, my son tells a desk clerk that he and Mommy just married Richard. The desk clerk tries to correct him. My son, in his young wisdom, explains to the man that we ALL got married and became a family.

When we finally arrive at our room, there is a gift basket filled with toys and a card that reads, "Congratulations to the three newlyweds."

The Birth of My First Child

All my life I was told how I bore a striking resemblance to my Aunt Evelyn. A few years before my birth, Evelyn and her unborn baby died when she became sick with pneumonia. It was a tragedy that was devastating to my Father and his family.

In 1974, I gave birth to my first child.

Unbeknownst to me, as I was in labor, my Father dressed very professionally, walked past the front desk and stood outside the delivery room. My Mother (who told me this story days later) said the staff assumed he was one of the Doctors and didn't question him.

My Father stood there for a very long time until he heard someone say, "It's a boy!", and his first born daughter exclaim, "I made a baby!!" Then he quietly walked away.

As my Mother shared this story with me, I felt SO loved to have a Father like him. A Father who stood outside my delivery room praying history would not repeat itself, with the daughter who bore such a likeness to his sister.

His prayers were answered.

A Special Friendship

I met Mara in the laundry room on the 14th floor of our apartment building. I had a baby attached to my hip, and she had three children huddled by her side. She looked like a tiny version of Sophia Loren. She was absolutely gorgeous.

Striking up a conversation, I found out she was from Brazil. Her English was limited, so the children contributed to the conversation. The family had moved to Miami Beach so the children could attend a Jewish day school.

Their Father was still in Brazil. I thought Mara was very brave to make such a big move for her children.

Mara and I quickly became inseparable. I discovered that someone was charging her an outrageous amount of money to tutor her children, and I offered to help them improve their reading skills.

Language arts were my area of expertise. It bothered me that someone was taking advantage of an immigrant who had no idea what things should cost in our country. She, in turn, was there for me and my baby boy.

Eventually we both moved to different areas of town. Mara's husband finally moved here permanently from Brazil. They chose to become Orthodox Jews and eventually had two more children.

One day Mara called, and we were reminiscing about the past.

She said, "Debi, do you remember all the fun we had spending time together when we lived down the hall from each other? I need to tell you something."

I couldn't imagine what she was going to say.

"Debi, I couldn't understand 95% of what you would be talking about. I would just nod and smile at you. What I figured out was... If I listened to you long enough I would eventually learn English. You know what? It worked!!"

My mind went back to all those thousands of hours of conversation, and I realized she was right!! I thought Mara just had difficulty expressing herself in English. I didn't realize she barely understood a single word I said!

I thought about how blessed I was to have met this woman. I was a new Momma and she showed me, by her unconditional love to her children, what was truly important. I doubt any words from her would have made a difference.

Friendship is a wonderful gift.

Yes Darling, She Got It From You

My Mother was not known for her culinary skills, though her five children never realized that until they left home. She made a lot of casseroles which we happily ate.

I remember being a twenty year old college student / newlywed standing in front of the meat counter at the grocery store. An older gentleman butcher came up to me and asked if I needed help. I looked at him with tears in my eyes and said, "I have no idea how to pick out meat."

He smiled and spent the next fifteen minutes explaining every cut to me and telling me how to cook it. When he realized my budget was more suited for the pasta aisle, he walked me to the less expensive cuts and taught me the meaning of the word "marinate".

On Thanksgiving, I bought a big turkey and followed directions in a cookbook. I thought I was doing a spectacular job until I went to lift it from the pan, and it collapsed into what felt like a million pieces. It was a big soggy mess.

My Mother gave her largest pieces of cookware to me when her five children left home. I was determined to show her what a terrific cook I was.

One night, when I was eight months pregnant with my second child, I hosted a dinner party. With my big belly wrapped in an adorable apron, I proudly brought her cookware to the table and waited for the *oohs* and *aahs* at the magnificent brisket I had prepared surrounded by potatoes and vegetables.

Everyone got busy eating. No one said a word about my food. I was very worried…

My Mother looked at me and smiled.

"She obviously got this talent for cooking from me. This is scrumptious!"

My Father, being the wise man that he was, looked at his gorgeous bride of thirty years and said, "Yes, darling, she got it from you!"

My Mother's Forever Love

Many years ago, my Mother and I attended an art show at our synagogue. As we took turns holding my infant son (her first grandchild), we marveled at all the beautiful artwork.

We came upon an artist completing a painting of a Mother and Child. The artist saw us watching her.

She said, "This is just my rough sketch. I am going to create a beautiful oil painting from this."

I turned to my Mother and said, "I think this is spectacular just the way it is. I wouldn't change a thing."

A few minutes later, my Mother excused herself to use the restroom. When she returned, she smiled at me and said, "I'm so happy you attended this show with me. Isn't it a gorgeous day?"

A few days later, my Mother called and asked me to stop by. When I got to her house, there was a beautifully wrapped package on the kitchen table.

"Let me hold the baby," she said. "Please open the package."

I tore off the gift wrapping and couldn't believe my eyes. There was the sketch framed in a flattering color that accentuated its beauty. I looked at my Mother, and her face was glowing.

"I wanted you to have this so you would always remember the day we spent together."

Sadly, it was one of the last Mother / Daughter outings we shared. Shortly after that, my beautiful, vibrant Mother became physically debilitated and was mostly homebound.

Looking at this artwork brings me such joy.

I feel my Mother's love in my home and forever in my heart.

Such a Love

In the late 70s, my husband was the property manager for several apartment buildings. I felt like I hit the jackpot when my husband's boss offered to rent us an apartment over twice the size of our tiny one. The rent was affordable, and it included a washer and dryer! What more could I ask for?

The apartment was a second floor walk-up. The neighbors upstairs had to walk by our apartment to get to theirs.

One day, a neighbor saw me getting ready to carry my newborn baby and toddler up the steps.

Offering to help me, she smiled and said, "I wasn't intentionally looking into your living room last night, but you had your blinds open. I saw you stretched out on your husband's lap and he was leaning over you, staring into your eyes. I was SO touched by the romantic scene. You're so blessed. I hope one day I can find a man who will love me like that!"

I thanked my next door neighbor for helping me upstairs. As I tucked the children in for their afternoon nap, I thought of the young woman's words. I did feel blessed. I had a husband who, after a hard day's work, spent fifteen minutes leaning over me, patiently trying to help me get an eyelash out of my eye. What a terrific guy!!

Did I tell my neighbor what she actually saw? Of course not!!

Like the Momma next door, she deserved to find her Prince Charming and live a wonderful life!

I Would Not Be Invisible

When my Mother began to show advanced symptoms of Parkinson's disease, it often caused her to become unbalanced, and she would stumble.

Some people looked at her as if she was drunk. She held on to me, and we ignored their stares. I was very proud to have my Mother by my side.

One day I took my Mother out to lunch, and it was challenging for her to hold the menu. The waiter paid no attention to my Mother as if she was invisible.

He turned to me and asked, "What does SHE want?"

I saw the look of sadness on my beautiful Mother's face.

I replied, "Please ask HER not me. She is perfectly capable of telling you!"

I helped her steady the menu in her hands as she made her selection.

We had a lovely lunch, and the incident was not mentioned. Sadly, soon my Mother's condition grew much worse and outings became a thing of the past.

Years after my Mother went to heaven, I was briefly afflicted with Bell's palsy, which made my face look like I had suffered a stroke. One day I was in a department store bathroom and a young woman walked in with a little girl. I turned to the woman and attempted to say, "She is adorable."

The words came out garbled and my face was contorted. The woman gave me a frightened look, grabbed the child's hand, and ran out of the bathroom.

I stood there crying. I looked at myself in the mirror and saw my Mother. Her soulful eyes stared back at me.

Closing my eyes, I felt her arms around me. I needed a hug from my Mother.

When I walked out that door with a lopsided smile, people stared... I didn't care.

Just like my beloved Mother.... I would not be invisible.

The Poetry Book

When my Mother was bedridden from a debilitating illness and trying desperately to keep her mind active, she would invite me to curl up next to her and read her my poetry.

One day she offers to help me "edit" my poetry. Over my next few visits, we go through every poem, and she makes her changes. Finally the task is completed!!

I climb into bed next to my Mother and she looks over her revisions and says, "Why would I ever think that your expressive poetry, that is so YOU, would need to be revised. Please ignore everything I added or deleted and put it all back the way you had it!"

She hands me back my book of poems knowing I won't question her decision. I feel validated as a writer and proud to be her daughter.

That afternoon, in a colorful new notebook with lots of blank pages, I write all my poems again in their original form.

All these years later, tucked away with my special things, I still have that "revised" poetry book with my Mother's handwritten notes. How could I ever throw it away?

I feel her love on every page.

I love you so much
We exchange thoughts
with our eyes
You are telling me
the time has come
To say our goodbyes.

~September 1991

My Father's Daughter

In the 1980s, my job as a summer day camp Director was like an extension of my role as a Mother. I always believed my success came from having the attitude that my campers should be treated with the same love that I gave to my own children.

One day, right before camp opened, I received a phone call from the synagogue office. I was being forewarned that a local politician's wife was coming to see me. She was insisting that her child be enrolled in my summer camp. The deadline for enrollment was long over, and there was a waiting list if someone cancelled.

The woman arrived moments later. She had already been told the camp was full. She strongly suggested I replace one of my scholarship students with her child. I gently but firmly explained that this would never happen. I had worked hard for months raising scholarship money from caring people in the community. These children, mostly immigrants, deserved a summer camp experience.

At that point she asked me, "Do you know who I am?"

I looked at her and smiled. "Yes I do, and I believe there are openings at another Jewish day camp. I would be happy to give you their phone number."

She stomped out of my office. I soon received a phone call that the Rabbi wanted to see me.

Our meeting went well. The Rabbi had officiated at my parents' wedding in 1947 and had tremendous respect for them. I knew he also respected the decisions I made for the children he had entrusted in my care. I believed that though there could be repercussions for my decision to NOT let an "influential" person intimidate me, he would support me.

I believed that because he was a *Mensch* (good person) and an incredible Rabbi.

As I was leaving, Rabbi smiled at me and said, "You are your Father's daughter."

Words I cherish to this day.

The Clock

I met Sophie when I was the Activities Director at a large synagogue in South Florida. She was a preschool teacher who was absolutely adored by the children and their parents. She had long, lustrous brown hair and the most expressive blue eyes. Her affection for her students was endearing.

One day I ask Sophie if she has a boyfriend, and she smiles and says, "I'm afraid I'm not the type of girl that men want to date."

She gives me a look that I immediately understand. As my Zaydie would say, she was a *gute medyl* (good girl).

That night I have a dream. In this dream, I see my butcher's son and Sophie together. Sam, who is a music teacher and single, has been helping his Father out in his spare time. Sam is extremely friendly and bears a resemblance to my husband - so what's not to like?

The next day I stop by the butcher and drop off a note for Sam. He laughs when he reads it.

"Sam... I have a gorgeous Jewish girl for you to meet. Don't worry she has a terrible personality."

(A little joke from the days when "she has a good personality" meant she might not be very attractive.)

Sam calls Sophie, and they go out on a date.

Then another, and another...

A few months later, my family and I are eating dinner, when there's a knock at the door. Standing there with a huge smile on her face is Sophie. Next to her is Sam, holding a wrapped box. I invite them in. Sophie shows me her manicured left hand. She's wearing a sparkling diamond ring.

"Thank you Jewish matchmaker! You found my soulmate." She gives me a huge hug.

Sam hands me the box which I open at the table. In it is a clock created from wood. Not only is it beautiful, it is exactly what I needed!!

Over thirty-five years later, this clock has traveled with me hundreds of miles to five different homes. I look at it dozens of times a day, always a constant reminder that there's nothing more priceless in the world than LOVE.

*Sophie saved the funny note that I wrote Sam. It is on the first page of their wedding album.

Wolfie's 21 Girl

My Father, Joseph Nevel, owned Wolfie's 21 on Miami Beach for the last eighteen years of his life. His charismatic personality made a big impact on his customers, and they all loved him.

Being fluent in Yiddish endeared him to his senior citizens who came in for their early bird daily fix of Jewish cuisine. Often the women would slip a few rolls and other goodies in their oversized purses to nosh on later. My Father insisted his staff act like they didn't notice, because in some cases he knew this was their main meal of the day.

One day my Father told me to come to the restaurant in a nice dress. He had a surprise for me. When I got there, he had a makeup artist and hairdresser waiting to transform me into a model. I was going to be the "Wolfie's Girl" for his advertising campaign.

The ads appeared in magazines all over the world, and it was framed by the front door. Here's the funny thing. No one (except family and close friends) ever knew it was me. I was Momma to four young children and usually wore my hair back in a ponytail with very little makeup.

It was exciting to be the Wolfie's Girl even though I was incognito!! (The young man sitting next to me was a part time actor who had appeared in Miami Vice.)

Another happy memory from Miami Beach.

Love Makes A Home

In 1987, we put our Miami Beach home on the market. We were relocating to North Carolina. People traipsed through our home with such serious faces, not acknowledging its excellent condition, but quick to point out minor flaws like a small crack in the original Cuban tile flooring.

Back then the house was already over fifty years old. Despite being an older home, it was built incredibly well.

"A hurricane couldn't blow this house down!" my husband used to say, every time he tried to hang a photo and couldn't get a nail through the cement walls. He was right!!

I was hoping folks would imagine the history of this home and the generations of children who grew up in it. I wanted them to feel the character and charm of yesteryear, not look at it as just some old house.

A young couple came into our home after admiring all the fruit trees in our beautiful yard. Their faces lit up. The wife turned to the husband and said, "I can feel the love in this home. This is where I want to raise our babies!"

I turned to my husband and said, "Accept whatever they offer!"

Love makes a home.

Mommy Has Gone To Heaven

On September 19th, 1991, my Father called me and said, "Your Mother has gone to heaven."

At first it didn't make any sense to me. My Mother had been severely disabled for many years and never went anywhere. How could she have gone to heaven?

My brain could not understand or accept that my Father was trying to soften the blow. There was silence on the phone.

Then he added, "Mommy closed her eyes forever while wrapped in my arms, exactly where she wanted to be."

I remember calling the airlines trying to get six last minute tickets to fly to Miami. Jewish funerals happened quickly. The woman on the phone started crying when she heard why I had to find those tickets! I never forgot her compassion toward me.

A friend owned a hotel on Miami Beach and generously offered me rooms for my large family. I remember standing at the window on the early morning of the funeral watching the sunrise. I've never forgotten that moment.

I sat next to my Father at the funeral service and held his hand.

Don't worry Daddy. I'll be strong for you. I'll hug all the family and friends and thank them for coming. I'm your oldest daughter and you can count on me.

This is what went through my head as I listened to the Rabbi speak about the incredible woman who brought me into this world.

Later, as my Mother's coffin was lowered into the ground, I felt a sorrow that crushed my heart.

At dusk, I stood by the ocean and cried as my world grew dark.

The Birthday Gift

After our beloved Mother (the gift buyer) passed away, our Father would give each of his five children a monetary gift for our birthdays and tell us to do something special for ourselves.

One year, I decided to take singing lessons. Though I had performed a little through the years, I never had any professional training.

I really liked the teacher. She was soft spoken and kind. At the first lesson, she had me sing a song and then she asked, "Do you always sing Alto?"

I explained to her that I felt very uncomfortable reaching for those high notes. She said I shouldn't give up without more effort. She gave me several exercises to do and told me to practice. (I did, every single day, which I'm sure the neighbors all heard.)

When my money ran out, I thanked the teacher for the lessons and told her they meant the world to me. I'm not sure my teacher realized that what I walked away with was SO much more than just ways to expand my vocal range.

I learned to step out of my comfort zone and not be afraid to challenge myself in other areas of my life. Like trying to reach those high notes, I may have shattered a few glasses along the way but I've always stepped over the pieces and kept on going.

I think my Father would be happy that his gift had such an impact on my life. He had such a magnificent voice. I hope he's singing in heaven.

Music touches the heart and the soul.

The Phone Call I Will Never Forget

In the late 70s, as the after school program Director for a synagogue, my job included helping the newly arrived Russian / Jewish teenagers get involved in after school activities. I created a fun-filled, stimulating program, and they had their choice of activities.

The teens and I immediately bonded. I told them how all four of my grandparents had emigrated from Russia (now Ukraine) and they immediately opened up about their lives. We had some really interesting conversations about the old country and how religious persecution still existed.

One afternoon, one of the boys stayed after hours to talk to me. He said he really needed a job, but no one would hire him. He told me his financial help was needed at home. I had observed that Daniel didn't socialize very much with the other boys, and I sensed he felt he didn't fit in.

I created a job for Daniel in our Youth Center and paid him out of my pocket. Every day he helped me keep the building clean. My parents, being kindhearted, hired him to do various chores around their house.

Fifteen years later, on the eighth night of Chanukah, the phone rang. A deep voice asked if this was Debi. I said "yes" wondering who it could be.

It was Daniel. He had called the synagogue earlier that day to try to find me. Someone informed him I had moved to North Carolina. Fortunately for him, they had my phone number.

Daniel said, "I want to thank you for giving me my first job. I also want you to know I attended college on a scholarship and went on to graduate school, and now I'm a psychologist."

He paused before saying something that brought tears to my eyes…

"You were there for me at the most challenging time of my life, and I have never forgotten you."

When I moved to North Carolina in 1987 and left the most amazing job I ever had, I thought I would never hear from my Russian students again. I was so anxious to know how life turned out for them. I wanted to know, if like my grandparents, they found their happiness in this country.

I received my answer as the flames of the Chanukah candles shed light upon my world.

I Can't Stay Silent Anymore

Many years ago, a history teacher from our local high school asked me to come in and speak with the students about the Holocaust. He was disturbed that the textbook the school system was using for his grade levels included only a few short paragraphs about this most important time in history.

The students were respectful, and after my history lesson, they asked a lot of questions. They had no idea about the horrors of the Holocaust. I kept my composure, but I was overwhelmed by their lack of knowledge. I understood why the teacher wanted a Jewish person to speak to the class.

When the class was dismissed, a student stayed behind. She told me that her grandfather, who lived with the family, was Jewish, but her parents said it was best that it never be mentioned to anyone.

She said, "I can't stay silent anymore. I am part Jewish, and according to what you taught us, I believe Hitler would have showed me no mercy. The thought that I, at sixteen, would have been murdered because I was a Jew shatters my heart."

I reached for her hand and told her she was very courageous to come forward. I welcomed her to the Jewish faith and told her I was always available if she wanted to talk.

Before she left, she told me she was going to have a long talk with her parents and grandfather. No more secrets.

I prayed their response was positive.

I wanted her to be proud to be a Jew.

Between Two Friends

When we started our business in 1991, James was our very first employee. My husband and James worked extremely long hours together until we had enough accounts to hire more staff.

A friendship was formed between Richard, a Jewish white man, the son of a Polish immigrant, and James, a Christian black man, the descendant of slaves. Both were family men steeped in their own traditions. Both had excellent work ethics.

One day James got very sick and was rushed to the hospital. He was giving the staff a hard time, and his wife called our home in desperation.

Richard went to the hospital, and a Doctor stopped him as he was about to enter his employee / friend's room.

"This floor only allows family to visit."

Without missing a beat, Richard replied, "I'm his brother."

The Doctor looked at Richard for a long moment, and then motioned him to go in.

James was very surprised to see him and started to complain about everything. Richard let him finish. Then he told James that there was no way he could afford to raise *his* family along with his own, so dying wasn't an option. He told him to stop being a stubborn old fool.

Then Richard leaned over the hospital bed and whispered something in his ear before leaving the room.

His wife said that from that moment on, James behaved like a real gentleman to the hospital staff. He made a great recovery.

When he came back to work, the incident was never mentioned again.

Years later, James went to take a nap in his favorite chair and never woke up. Sadly, it was his young granddaughter who found him lifeless.

At his funeral, my husband leaned over his casket and said something I couldn't hear.

I asked him what he said to James and he replied, "That's between two friends."

A good friend is like a brother.

Rest in peace, James.

I'm Married To A Movie Star

Many years ago, our local newspaper ran a story about a movie that was being filmed in our town. The story said children and adults were needed for minor roles. One of our daughters decided she would love the opportunity to audition. The family accompanied her to the casting call.

When we arrived at the Great Smokies Hilton, we were informed that the newspaper had printed incorrect information. The talent scouts were only looking for adults for various roles. The children's roles had already been filled.

Hubby was standing in a corner with his arms folded across his chest watching all the activity. A talent scout approached him and asked if HE would like to do a very short screen test.

According to her, there might be a part for him in the movie. The family encouraged him, so he agreed.

With the camera rolling, the talent scout asked him a few questions, which he answered without a problem. Then she asked him his phone number for a potential callback.

His mind went completely blank, and he asked, "Debi, what's my phone number?"

Everyone laughed at his "stage fright" including the cameraman.

A few days later, hubby got a callback, and he was offered a (non-speaking) role as a security guard in the movie, which was being filmed at the magnificent Biltmore Estate.

He and the other local actors mingled with the celebrities during the breaks and were treated to delicious catered buffets. It was such an exciting experience!

The movie, called Richie Rich, came out on December 21st, 1994.

For weeks after the movie played in our town, children would recognize Richard and come running up to him. He was a local celebrity!!

So now you know...

I'm married to a movie star.

My 30 Seconds Of Fame

Many years ago when we lived on the side of a mountain, a family of bears decided to make our driveway their new home. The baby bears climbed up one of our trees. Papa Bear took off, leaving Momma Bear to watch the babies.

We couldn't leave our home or walk to our cars because Momma Bear was standing in front of them. Her face threatened... "Don't even think of coming anywhere near me because I will make chopped liver out of you!"

Eventually animal control and the Sheriff's department came. They blocked off the road. Once it was very quiet, the baby bears came down from the tree and sauntered off with Momma Bear.

The local news station came by to interview us. For a small town, this was a BIG story.

The next morning, we were eating breakfast, watching Good Morning America. One of the hosts said, "Up next we have a bear story!"

Kidding around I said to my husband, "WE have a bear story worth sharing!"

After the commercial, the bear story came on. IT WAS OUR STORY!! They were sharing the story from our local TV station. Within minutes, relatives and friends were calling from all over the country asking us if we knew we were on national television. It was SO exciting!!

If I had known that our bear story was going to be seen around the country, I would have dressed up in a fabulous outfit and worn my brightest lipstick for the interview. After all, it was my big thirty seconds of fame.

The Very Special Anniversary

I'm going through my wallet, and I find the card. I have carried it since our 25th Anniversary.

I love you more and more each day. Love, Richard

I remember the moment like it was yesterday. I walked into the hotel room, and there were two dozen gorgeous red roses with a note attached.

I looked at my husband, and his eyes spoke volumes. He had planned this trip down to the very last detail.

We rarely take vacations because of our family owned business, and this trip was SO important to him. It was his way of showing how much he cares about "us" with all that we've been through together.

Everything about those two days was perfect.

We fell in love again.

My husband just called me as he was driving through the mountains from one job to the next.

He asked me what I'm doing.

I told him I'm organizing my wallet.

The Dancer

As a child, my Mother enrolled me in various dance classes. She knew I loved writing poetry and stories, and she wanted me to have another outlet for creative expression.

Ballet was difficult for me. The teacher was rigid, never smiled, and preferred the graceful, petite girls.

Tap dancing was fun and not as restrictive. I quickly mastered the routines and taught them to my younger siblings. My absolute favorite was modern jazz. I imagined myself on Broadway dancing in a musical!!

As I grew older, I stopped taking classes, but was appreciative of my Mother introducing me to all types of dance.

Twenty-five years later, I volunteered to create a dance troupe in our local elementary school. Our school was one of the oldest in the city, and many of the children couldn't afford to take extracurricular activities.

My troupe quickly filled up with girls and boys. Rehearsals were hectic but exciting, and finally we were ready for our first performance! It took place in the parking lot of a local mall. The kids were fantastic and the audience cheered.

My dancers moved on to middle school. A few years later, a new elementary school was built, and a wealthy benefactor contributed a large amount of money to create a dance troupe with fancy costumes and performances in classy places. I felt sad that my dancers didn't have those same opportunities.

One day a few years ago, a man who looked to be in his early 40s approached me in a restaurant and said, "I hope you remember me. I was in your dance troupe back in 6th grade. I was the kid who gave you a hard time because I thought dancing was just for girls. You told me it was fine to just sit and watch. Then I got bored sitting by myself and joined the troupe."

"I do remember you. You turned out to be a terrific dancer!"

He laughed. "That's because you made it fun!! It's great to see you after all these years. Hope you're still dancing!!"

I watched as he joined his wife and children at a table. Finishing dinner, I walked out to the parking lot and danced my way to the car.

Kindness of a Stranger

My husband and I had gone back and forth from North Carolina several times in the past six weeks, making the thirty hour (round trip) drive just to spend precious last moments with my Father.

Exhausted, we stopped at a diner in the early morning for some breakfast. My tears fell into my coffee as I talked about the Father I adored and all my sweet memories of him.

My husband reached across the table and took my hand. "He will never be forgotten. You'll make sure of that."

As we started to leave, a man stood up and blocked us. I knew he was part of a motorcycle group that had come in right after us.

"I can't let you leave without telling you that I overheard your conversation. I know your Dad is dying, and I want you to know that we are going to pray for you."

I looked up at this big, burly man who might have intimidated me under different circumstances. I reached up and gave him a hug and felt the strength of his words flow through me.

As we drove away, all I could think was...

It is wonderful to show kindness to a stranger.

The Tape

After my Father passed away, I discovered a tape tucked amongst his possessions. He had left me a box filled with things he knew would be meaningful to me.

As soon as I started listening to the tape, I realized it was my Mother who had died many years ago. She had recorded the tape before she lost the ability to communicate. It was recorded in increments and was a diary of her illness. With each addition to the tape, I could hear her voice getting weaker and weaker until it was barely audible.

I listened to my Mother talk about her daily physical struggles. She spoke of the sorrow she felt being such a burden to my Father, and how she adored him and believed he deserved so much better. You could hear the anguish in her voice.

Sitting alone, I played that tape a dozen times cradling my arms around my tape recorder as if it would erase all the years and bring me back home. I wanted to hold my precious Mother and take away all her unhappiness and pain.

Outside the window
I could hear the rain
showering the earth with my tears.

I am grateful my Father entrusted me with my Mother's tape. I imagine his heartache when he heard the love of his life's last words. Being the caring person he was, in his final years, he never shared his sadness, choosing to live each day loving his family and spreading happiness.

May they both rest in peace.

FAMILY & FRIENDS

How Bubbi & Zaydie Met

It was the early 1900s and a young man comes from Kiev, Russia to the United States so that he can start a new life without religious persecution. He leaves behind his young wife and two little daughters.

The young immigrant works day and night saving every penny. Finally he has enough money to bring his family to the United States.

When his young wife receives the tickets for the journey, she is SO excited she scoops up her little girls and runs down the road to her parents' house. As she opens their door, she collapses and dies.

The young man is overwhelmed with grief. His in-laws temporarily take care of his daughters while he works even harder saving money to bring them over, too.

Time passes... One day he sees a *maidel* (young woman), and he can't believe his eyes. She looks exactly like his deceased wife. He gets up the courage to speak to her and discovers she is very intelligent and also a Russian immigrant. She is in her early twenties and single.

On their first date, the young man comes to the back door to pick her up. He doesn't want to make her feel uncomfortable about dating a widower.

The young woman flashes her dark brown eyes at him and says, "I am NOT embarrassed to be seen with you. Now please come to my front door!!"

The couple fall in love and get married. The wife becomes a loving stepmother to his two daughters. They have seven more children.

This is the story of my beloved paternal Zaydie and Bubbi.

As a child, I was very blessed to have both of them in my life.

My Father's Passion For Yiddish

My Father was raised in Chicago and only spoke Yiddish until he was five years old. His first day of Kindergarten, his older sisters walked him to school and made sure he got safely to his classroom.

At recess, he was beat up by older bullies on the playground for being a "Yid" who couldn't speak English.

My Father never let that happen again. He made it his mission to become the most articulate English speaking student in the class. He was an accomplished student and ended up skipping a grade and graduating high school early.

He had a passion for the Yiddish language and stayed fluent in Yiddish all his life by working as a translator for various writers.

My Father never allowed his five children to abuse the English language. Cursing was frowned upon, as were slang words. Dinner conversations were always stimulating and lively.

My Father's influence along with my Mother's exquisite way of expressing herself inspired me to become a human interest writer.

A Letter To My Aunt Elizabeth

Dear Elizabeth,

This is your niece, Debi, writing to you one hundred years after your death. I hope my words find their way to heaven.

My Father, your little brother, always described you so eloquently:

"A beautiful child with golden hair."

My father told me that after having measles as a child, you developed severe heart trouble and grew weaker every day until you had no strength to fight anymore.

When you died at only ten years old, your parents were consumed with grief. Your Mother sobbed as your Father threw himself over your casket pleading with G-d to take HIM not you.

No parent should have to bury their child. I cry thinking about my beloved Zaydie being in such emotional pain.

Growing up, I wanted to know everything about you... every detail of your short life. My Father brought you back to life for me with his childhood stories. He loved you so much.

Elizabeth... My beautiful Aunt with the golden hair...

I'm sorry I didn't have the joy of knowing you.

I hold you close in my heart forever.

With love,

Debi

Spunky Aunt Annie

Annie was one of my Father's seven sisters. She was an attractive brunette with a smile that could light up a room.

As a young woman, she was offered a job as a server at an elegant hotel on South Beach.

One night she was serving drinks and appetizers to a group of young businessmen. They were deep in conversation when she leaned over the table to place their drinks and hors d'oeuvres in front of them.

One of them said in Yiddish to the others, "She looks yummy. I wouldn't mind taking a little bite out of her!"

They all laughed.

Unbeknownst to the men, my Aunt Annie was fluent in Yiddish. She backed up from the table and flashed them a dazzling smile.

She said, "*Jentlmen, gut glik. Dos vet keynmol pasirn.*" ("Gentleman, good luck. That will NEVER happen!!")

The look of shock on their faces was priceless. They had no idea that their adorable server was a spunky Jewish girl. Nor did they realize she was the niece of the owner of the hotel.

After they left, Annie found an enormous tip on the table from the very embarrassed group of men.

Shortly after, Annie met and married a charming Jewish man from Tennessee, where she learned to speak Yiddish with a southern accent.

Unconditional Love

A hundred years ago, my great Uncle, who was raised Orthodox, married a gentile, and the adult family members of that generation shunned him. He was never talked about. It was as if he never existed.

When I was growing up, I watched my Father reach out to his Uncle's son and create a lifelong friendship with him. His cousin was not raised as a Jew, but it made no difference to my Father. He was family and that was all that mattered.

This unconditionally love that I witnessed was one of many things I learned from my Father. He embraced every member of our family regardless of their religious affiliation. The only thing he cared about was keeping us close-knit.

Twenty years have passed since my beloved Father went to heaven. I believe if he was here today, he would be reaching out to every member of our extended family, from the Orthodox Jews living in Israel to the grandchildren of family members who are being raised outside our faith.

My Father, the wise sage of our family, would continue to make everyone feel special. He would give them a sense of pride in being a member of our family.

He would make sure they never forgot their Jewish roots by setting an example of absolute love.

The Road Trip

In the mid-40s, my Father took a road trip with his Mother from Chicago to Miami. My Father was helping relocate his parents and many of his siblings to beautiful South Florida.

As they drove through South Carolina, they heard sirens, and a Sheriff pulled them over.

"Going a little fast there boy," the officer said to my Father.

"Sir, I wasn't speeding. I have my Mother in the car, and I was following all the traffic rules."

"Be quiet," the officer growled. "You can pay this ticket right now or go to jail. We don't put up with outsiders breaking rules in this town!"

My Bubbi was frightened and whispered to her son in Yiddish, "I don't understand what is happening!"

My Father calmly told her that he would explain everything later.

They were taken to the "courthouse" where a judge (conveniently available) found my Father guilty of speeding. He was instructed to pay a hefty fine.

My Father knew it was a dishonest scheme, but was wise enough to know when to keep his mouth shut. He paid the money, and they continued on their journey.

When my Father told me this story many years later, he said my Bubbi, who was greatly traumatized by acts of hate she witnessed in Russia, was afraid they would be murdered, and no one would ever find their bodies.

My heart hurts for the fear she must have felt.

The Neighbor

In 1947, when my parents married, they rented a small apartment in Miami.

One day, my Mother was hanging her wet laundry on the clothesline behind the building and an older woman gave her a mean look and said, "Get your clothes off our line you Kike."

My Mother at twenty-three had never been called an offensive name for a Jew and stared at the woman with sadness in her eyes. She took her basket of clothes and went back to her apartment.

When my Father came home from work, she told him what happened. His face got flushed, but as was his temperament, he didn't respond with anger. He went to pay a visit to the elderly neighbor.

When he returned, he said to my Mother, "Go outside and hang our wet laundry on the clothesline. Our neighbor apologizes for what she said and will never disrespect you again."

When my Father shared this story with me, I pleaded with him to tell me what he said to the neighbor.

He smiled at me and replied...

"Sometimes in life, it is better to approach a situation with concern for the person who is SO miserable that they feel it necessary to lash out at others. Whatever I said to her remains between the two of us. The important thing to remember is... If you treat others with kindness and respect, you've set an example that you hope they will follow."

Another great lesson I learned from my Father.

The Nevelsky Brothers

The Nevelsky brothers, children of Russian immigrants, were eleven years apart. Joseph was the first son, born after several sisters, and Sam was the "surprise" baby born to their Mother when she was in her early forties.

Joseph adored his baby brother and was like a second Father to him. As they grew up, the bond between them grew even stronger.

After Sam got out of the service and graduated college, he worked for his brother. Eventually, with his big brother's encouragement, he went out on his own and became very successful.

The love between these two brothers set a shining example for our family.

Joseph was my Father.

After my Father died in 2002, my Uncle Sam would call me and describe his vivid dreams. I could hear him sobbing.

"I felt my brother's breath against my neck as he hugged me. He hasn't left me. He's an Angel watching over me."

I would reassure my Uncle that he would always "feel" my Father's loving and gentle spirit. I reminded him that love is forever.

There are times in life, when we become nurturers to those who, in our childhoods, were there for us.

Dos iz lebn.

(This is Life.)

Sam walked the stairway to heaven in 2018.

My beloved Father was waiting...

Look For The Good

When I was a little girl, my Father shared so many family stories with me.

One story was about an Aunt of his who was always angry at everyone in our very large family. She bore grudges for years, never laying them to rest.

As the years went by, her immune system weakened, and she caught every illness one can imagine. Eventually she became so frail, her body couldn't fight anymore.

My Father, who always looked at life as a "half-filled" glass told me the story and added his thoughts.

"If you go through life always looking for the worst in people, that is exactly what you shall find. Everyone has their flaws, but they also have good qualities worth searching for, even if they are hidden behind their anger or pain."

Those words have stayed with me through the years.

I believe to stay physically and emotionally healthy, we have to imagine throwing our grudges to the wind and love each other unconditionally.

I never met my Father's Aunt. She died before I was born.

I wish her life had been happier and she had lived longer. It would have been another family member to love.

The Cooking Pot

The only physical thing I inherited from my Grandma Dorothy was a big cooking pot. Grandma passed down this cooking pot to my Mother Bracha, who handed it down to me.

The year is 1934 and ten year old Bracha is hiding behind the sofa giggling at her older brother who's sitting with his girlfriend. Her older twin sisters are in the kitchen helping their Mother prepare a special dinner.

At the butcher earlier in the day, Dorothy purchases a prime cut of meat. This is the first time her son has brought a girl home. Dorothy cooks a delicious pot roast and serves it with fresh vegetables bought from the vegetable stand next to the butcher. She arranges them attractively on a separate platter.

The year is 1964. Bracha is cooking a beef stew for dinner in the same big pot. She adds an assortment of vegetables and baby potatoes purchased at the grocery store. Bracha calls the five children to the table and reminds them to wash their hands. She doles out hearty portions, making sure each plate includes equal amounts of meat. There will be plenty for seconds.

The year is 1994. Debi is making sweet and sour meatballs in the same big pot. She's using ground turkey because she read it was healthier. The four children take their seats at the big wooden table. They can't wait to eat the extra-large meatballs on a plateful of noodles with lots of golden raisins. There will be sandwich fixings left over for tomorrow.

One day soon, this big cooking pot will be handed down to a child of the next generation. Inside the pot, they will find a written story of the three families who enjoyed meals lovingly prepared by their Mother, Grandmother and Great Grandmother.

It is not an heirloom valued at a large sum of money.

It is a cooking pot almost a hundred years old.

After reading the story, they will understand how...

It is worth so much more.

Aunt Shirley

The best way to describe Aunt Shirley is marvelously eccentric.

I loved everything about my Mother's older sister including her "space shoes" that a shoemaker had molded to fit her feet. They were the funniest looking shoes, but she never complained about her feet hurting.

Shirley lived on Miami Beach, and because of the heat and humidity, styled her thick curly hair very short. Clothing never interested her so she wore the same outfits for decades.

Shirley and I were kindred spirits. Once when my parents went away on a mini vacation, she moved in to our house to watch over the five children.

That week I had my first awakening into "womanhood," and she allowed me to skip school. We sipped tea all day and talked about this next exciting stage of my life.

At twelve, I was overwhelmed with gratitude for this woman who never married, but was like a second Mother to me.

When I moved to North Carolina thirty-five years ago, Shirley wrote me long beautifully composed letters from the retirement home where she resided. She made every detail of her days sound newsworthy. I devoured her letters, hungry for news from home.

I responded to every one of Shirley's letters, sharing what it was like to live in a small town in the mountains and telling her all our family's everyday activities.

When Shirley peacefully passed away, the retirement home sent me a package.

Wrapped in a pretty ribbon was every letter I had ever written my beloved Aunt.

Aunt Betty's Mitzvah

My Mother's older sisters were twins named Betty and Shirley. Neither ever married or had children, but they were devoted to their nieces and nephews. I can't remember a time in my life that they weren't there for me.

When my paternal Bubbi died in 1958, they were by my side, gently explaining to a distressed seven year old how I would always have my precious memories of her to comfort me. They held me in their arms and let me cry.

Betty had a successful career in New York City. When she was diagnosed with a condition that had no cure, she returned to South Florida, and Shirley became her caregiver. I loved spending time with both of them.

In 1987, I told my Aunties that I was moving to North Carolina. Though they were sad to see me go, they never made me feel anything but excited about this new beginning in my life.

One day as I was packing boxes, Shirley called. I knew from her voice something was terribly wrong.

"Betty died this morning," she said. "We were sitting on the porch, and she closed her eyes. I thought she had fallen asleep. She never woke up."

I will never forget that moment. The box I was packing fell from my hands, and I sat on the floor and sobbed.

Two days later, I found an envelope from Betty in my mailbox. Inside was a beautiful card with a check.

The card read, "Dear Debi, Please use this money for traveling expenses for you and the family. I wish you the happiest future. With all my love, Aunt Betty."

My beloved Aunt's last act on this earth was to do a *Mitzvah* (good deed) for her niece.

A Special Cousin

Paul was my Mother's cousin. As a child he lived with my Mother and her family for several years. My Mother adored her cousin Paul and considered him one of her best friends.

I always enjoyed when my Mother reminisced about their childhood and all the good times they shared. She told me that in his younger years, Paul had been a boxer. I found this fascinating because he was such a gentle, loving man, not aggressive at all. I couldn't imagine him being in a boxing ring.

Paul had a daughter who was close to my age. One night when I was eleven, my parents took us to the theater. We had a lovely time together. Soon after, she passed away from Leukemia.

I was never told that she was sick and was heartbroken. My parents did not take me to her funeral. I was confused why they made that decision. Years later, they explained they were trying to protect me from experiencing grief at such an early age. Looking back, I wished they had allowed me to go.

My Mother, her sister Betty and their cousin Paul were all afflicted with Parkinson's Disease. They were Ashkenazi Jews, and studies are being done to understand how this disease runs in families.

I named my youngest son in memory of my Mother's older brother, Paul, who passed away before my son was born. He was also a gentle, loving man adored by the family.

Two men I am proud to honor.

The Penny Jar

My Grandfather Herman was one of the best friends I ever had. He was almost deaf, and I was a chatterbox, which made us quite compatible.

We used to like to hang out together. We'd go to lunch, where he would tell me that I was his favorite grandchild every time. (Do you think my offering to pay for lunch may have been the reason I was ranked #1 grandchild?)

After lunch, he would show me off to all his cronies, who were gathered on the big porch of the apartment building on South Beach where he lived.

When I gave birth to my first born son, I was living just a short distance from Grandpa Herman's apartment. He had been diagnosed with Leukemia, and his health was rapidly failing. I came to visit often, knowing that spending time with my baby boy would bring him joy.

Grandpa Herman used to collect pennies in a big jar. One day, when it was just about filled, he told me to take the jar home. I looked at him and asked, "Why?" He said he wanted my son to have the money for his first birthday!

Just a few weeks later, for my twenty-fourth birthday, Grandpa Herman gave me $25… one dollar for every year, with an extra one for good luck. My Aunt Shirley helped him write out the card. He insisted on using lots of colored magic markers. (She told me later, that it took my grandfather hours to create the card.) I thanked my grandfather for the generous gift and the beautiful birthday card.

Later that afternoon, I walked with my baby in the stroller to Burdines to buy myself a new dress with my birthday money. I found the perfect one! It was a turquoise color with a swirly skirt. I couldn't wait to show my grandfather the gorgeous dress that he bought me!

My beloved Grandpa Herman died a few days later. I wore the turquoise dress to his funeral.

I know Grandpa would have loved it.

Worthy of Love

One of my cousins was born brain damaged from a forceps birth. Though I was quite young, my parents explained to me in language that I could understand, how he was not able to function like a healthy child, but still needed lots of love.

We would go visit him often at the special school where he lived. The attendants would carry him out to the visiting area with such gentleness and put him down next to us.

My Father would say, "Talk to him just like you talk to your siblings. Don't be afraid to stroke his *keppie*. He knows you're here and he feels your love."

I was eleven when my Mother's best friend came to visit with her nephew who had cerebral palsy. My Mother asked me to take him for a walk while she and her friend shared some grownup conversation.

I took his hand and off we went to explore the neighborhood. We talked nonstop. At the end of our walk, before getting into his Aunt's car for the ride home, he asked if he could kiss my cheek. I said "yes" and before the kiss, he whispered in my ear, "Thank you for treating me like a regular person. People rarely do."

I waved goodbye as the car drove off thinking about his words...

He was so much more than just a "regular" person.

He was a human being worthy of love.

My Angel

I met Eddie at a memorial service for a young friend who died from a brain tumor. She was busy serving punch but looked up and flashed me a radiant smile. I smiled back, and we started chatting. Eddie had been married to an older widowed man who was a brilliant scientist. She never had any children of her own. Her husband had died a few years earlier.

Very spontaneously I asked, "Would you adopt me?"

She laughed, and it sounded like beautiful, tinkling wind chimes. "Of course I will, darling girl!!"

Thus began a friendship between Eddie and a Mother of four who needed to fill a void in her heart. It was a wonderful friendship.

Months later, Eddie's cancer returned like an unwanted guest. I took it upon myself to organize visits from friends and food drop offs so all her needs would be met.

Eddie's stepchildren never visited her once, but my four children surrounded her with love. She died feeling like she had the daughter and grandchildren she always wanted.

Before Eddie went to heaven, she offered me her vehicle. She knew we were a one car family for the six of us. She owed $500 to pay the car off. We scraped the money together and gave it to Eddie which helped with her medical bills.

Shortly after Eddie's funeral, an elderly man ran a stop sign and smashed into the driver's side of the car. I was alone in the car. I lost control, and the car went spiraling toward a bridge. I felt Eddie take over the steering wheel. I felt her breath against my neck. I heard her sweet voice.

"Dear Debi," she whispered, "Today is not your day to die."

When the police found me hunched over my steering wheel in shock, I heard one say to his partner, "This woman must have an Angel. Her car stopped inches from that bridge. She would have been killed if the car had not stopped!"

There are Angels among us. Mine is named Eddie.

My Father-in-Law

Samuel Drecksler emigrated from Poland as a young person. He became a successful businessman who could converse in Polish, Yiddish and English. As I heard through the family grapevine, he was strikingly handsome and quite popular with the women.

The story goes that in the mid-1940s, when Samuel met my mother-in-law, Annie, he attempted to charm her into a relationship. At nineteen years old (ten years younger than Samuel), Annie was beautiful and had no problem speaking up.

She told her handsome suitor, "If you want me, put a ring on my finger."

They soon were married. Four boys followed. Samuel really wanted a daughter, but Annie was told having more children would jeopardize her health.

Sadly, Samuel had a heart condition. His first of four heart attacks happened shortly after they were married.

One night he fell asleep in bed cuddling with his two youngest sons. He never woke up. Annie was left a widow at thirty-nine.

I truly believe in divine intervention. Shortly before he died, Samuel stopped on the way home from a business trip to pay a surprise visit to Howard, his first born son, who was enrolled in college. It was the last time they'd see each other.

After Samuel died, my husband went to synagogue every single morning before going to school for one year to honor his Father. Since his older brother was away at college, at only fifteen years old, he stepped into the role of man of the house, taking care of his Mother and two younger brothers.

A few years later, when Howard was tragically killed by a drunk driver, it was my husband who handled everything. His Mother's heart was shattered into a million pieces.

My husband always told me how much his Father would have loved me. I wish I could go back in time and meet Samuel. I would give him a big hug and tell him that he finally got the daughter he wanted, and I will always keep his memory alive.

A Letter To My Brother

Dear Big Brother,

The other day when you called, we had a marvelous conversation walking down memory lane together. Growing up in the 50s and 60s, only twenty-one months apart in age, we always enjoy reminiscing about our childhoods. Such happy times!

It was always, "David and Debi". We were the amazing duo!! There's nothing we couldn't accomplish as long as we had each other!

When I miss our Father, I can look at a photo of you and see those same sparkling eyes and loveable smile. Not only do you resemble him physically, you have his good heart and gentle spirit.

Just like our Father, you always look at life as a "half-filled" glass. No matter what *tzuris* (trouble) you have dealt with in your lifetime, you never complain.

Your favorite phrase is, "Tomorrow will be better!"

Thank you for being such a positive influence in my life and for being such as wonderful role model. Every child should be blessed with a brother like you.

I love you more than I could ever express.

Your little sister,

Debi

"He who is full of joy is full of love." —Baal Shem Tov

Remembering Bubbi

Bubbi died when I was seven, but I remember her vividly.

She adored my Father, her first born son, and the feeling was mutual. Her greatest joy was talking with him in Yiddish.

Though I only understood a few words of their conversations, I could always tell by Bubbi's demeanor that she was extremely happy to spend time with him.

When my parents first got married, Bubbi and Zaydie would come over to check the kitchen and make sure my Mother was keeping kosher. My maternal Grandparents had not raised her as religious, so my Mother had much to learn. Bubbi never disrespected my Mother, choosing instead to patiently explain everything to her. They got along splendidly and were close until the day Bubbi's heart failed. She died in our home with both my parents by her bedside.

I remember Bubbi being soft and cuddly and having the scent of Jewish cooking on her clothes. There are days I wish I had bottled that smell.

Now that I am older, I look in the mirror and often see my Bubbi's image staring back at me. I feel such a strong connection... Not just our physical similarities, but a feeling of belonging to a family so steeped in love.

I feel blessed to have known my Bubbi even for a short time. She touched my life in such a positive way.

If I close my eyes, I hear her gentle voice whispering...

"Trag meyn zkhrun mit dir aoyf eybik."

("Carry my memory with you forever.")

MODERN DAY

The Momma

I saw her walking through the grocery store with a baby strapped to her chest, a toddler sitting in the front of the cart and two by her side.

She stopped at the juice aisle and gave me a grateful smile as I offered to reach up on a shelf and get her down a few bottles of apple juice. I recognized that smile. It was me several decades ago.

Her toddler was busy trying to open a bag of cookies and demanded her attention. I watched as she handled it without raising her voice or getting upset.

We met again outside as the older children were helping her put the grocery bags into the back of the car. She was thanking them for being such great helpers.

"Beautiful family. You're doing a great job!!"

She looked up at me and said, "I needed to hear that today. I just got the news that my Mother is sick and the prognosis isn't good."

The hurt on her face overwhelmed me. I painfully remembered receiving that news so many decades ago.

Without giving it a second thought, I gave this complete stranger a big hug, even though we've been told over and over again to keep our distance from each other.

The only thing this beautiful Momma would catch from me was a BIG dose of love.

And...

Love has no germs.

The Love Notes

I think of Valentine's Day as another day to acknowledge love, something we need more of in this world.

In the early 1900s, Hallmark started creating hundreds of Valentine's Day cards to choose from. Other companies followed. The cards were everything from very romantic verse to schmaltzy sayings to funny lines. I've always wondered how the companies decided which terms of endearment were worthy of inclusion.

As a writer, I might have missed my calling. I could see myself spending countless hours curled up in front of my fireplace writing poetic verse that would bring happiness to others.

I imagine someone saying, "Oh darling, these words just touch my heart!"

(Yes, I love old romance movies.)

My hubby never forgets the holiday. Every Valentine's Day for forty-five years, I've received three beautiful cards. I wake up to the cards lined up on the living room table. I love peeking at him while I'm opening the cards and reading them aloud. His eyes speak volumes.

Just as meaningful to me, during the "off holiday" season, he leaves me little hand written notes that put a smile on my face. I've saved every one of them in a shoebox.

I think it's the simple little acts of kindness that add a sweet flavor to life.

And I believe, every day is a perfect day to say…

Ikh hab dikh lib.
(I love you.)

*A Jewish holiday called Tu B'Av is often referred to as the Jewish day of love. In Israel, music and dance festivals are often held, and Israelis enjoy giving cards and flowers to their loved ones.

The Jewish Mother

It doesn't matter how old your child is, a Jewish mother will get a little *meshuge* (crazy) if she gets that call, "I don't feel well!"

It isn't necessary for her to have a medical degree because the day that child is born, she is infused with more knowledge than any specialist on this planet.

No one knows this child like she does!!

She will compile a list of every healing method and immediately send it to the child. It will include recipes from wise relatives long gone, what to add to the bath water and advice to have someone kiss his *keppie* every hour for a true temperature reading.

The phone will be left on all night long just in case Momma is needed at 3 a.m. Of course it will be by her side of the bed.

Promises will be made to G-d that if the child is healed, she will stop scavenging the kitchen cabinets for left over Halloween candy.

When she finally gets the call that her child has made a miraculous recovery, she acts SO calm on the phone, the child wonders if she flavored her morning coffee with schnapps.

She hangs up and kisses his photo reminiscing how fast those years went by.

Wasn't it just yesterday, he was a little boy?

My Three Gifts Next Door

There is something so precious about young children. They have no filters and say exactly what's on their minds.

I was talking to the young Momma next door, thanking her for the squash, zucchini and cucumbers she had left by my front door. Her sister has a garden, and it was overflowing with produce.

As we talked, two of her three little boys lifted my wrist and said, "You have beautiful bracelets!"

I smiled and told them the story behind each of them.

As they listened intently, I shared how both bracelets meant the world to me. One was the last gift I ever received from my Dad before he went to heaven. The other bracelet, my Dad had bought for my Mother many years ago when she was very sick and confined to her bed.

I told them how wearing both bracelets made me feel SO close to both my Mommy and Daddy, though they were not alive anymore.

The boys looked up at me with eyes so filled with light.

"I love that story," the oldest one said.

"Me, too," said his little brother.

The baby brother just grinned and wanted to touch the bracelets.

As I walked away, they called out the two favorite expressions I taught them from my 1950s childhood.

"See you later, Alligator."

"See you in a while, Crocodile."

I turned, laughed and waved goodbye to my three "gifts" next door.

Crumbled Cakes & All

I baked a cake, and it came out almost perfect. I couldn't wait to show Hubby when he came home from work.

After he enjoyed a slice, I asked him if it tasted better than the hundreds of other cakes I've baked through the decades, none as flawless as this one.

He smiled at me and said, "All your cakes have been delicious, even the ones that fell apart. If I refused to eat the less than perfect ones, I would have missed out on some real sweetness."

I looked at this man who for forty-five years has shared all my *simchas* (joys) and weathered all life's storms with me. My heart overflowed with love.

I remember when he asked my Father for my hand in marriage, and my Father smiled and replied, "Don't you want the rest of her?"

He said, "Yes, crumbled cakes and all."

Bonus Family

Having bonus family is a beautiful gift. Though you may not be related, the bond is so strong, it makes sense to call them family.

My best friend, an Orthodox Jew, has eleven children. When my youngest son was a little boy, he assumed they were our cousins. We were inseparable.

I love all of my friend's children but have a very special relationship with one daughter. There aren't enough words to describe how much she means to me.

When Rachel got married in 2008, she insisted my husband and I be in her family photos. She told us that one day we would be honorary Zaydie and Bubbi to her children.

She kept her word, and her son and daughter have been a big part of our lives. Though we live hundreds of miles from each other, not a week goes by that we don't text, send photos or speak on the phone.

I once asked my best friend if she minded that I "adopted" one of her daughters and two of her grandchildren.

She said, "Debi, I have SO many children, grandchildren and now great grandchildren. Do you want a few more?"

I would take them all.

"Who finds a faithful friend, finds a treasure."
~ Jewish Proverb

The Dream

It is after midnight and I'm upstairs in my office writing another story. I hear the train, as I do every night. The rhythmic sounds are music to my ears and make me sleepy... so so sleepy.

I'm running down my driveway toward the train, and I hear the conductor call out to me, "Hold on a minute. We'll slow down and you can come aboard!"

A gentleman reaches for my hand and helps me up the steps. I take a seat and ask, "Where is this train going, Sir?"

He replies in a gentle voice, "Anywhere you want young lady!"

I start to say, "I'm not a young lady anymore," but then looking at him, I discover that he is MUCH older than me. He seems to be about 135 years old. I stare at him very closely and realize it is my Zaydie!!

"Zaydie Nevelsky!! It is so wonderful to see you again. What brings you down from heaven?"

"I thought my granddaughter could use a visit."

"Zaydie, let's go on an adventure together!!"

"*Ikh vel dikh nemen aoyf a kurtse nsyeh aber dan muztu geyn aheym!*"

("I will take you on a short trip but then you have to go home!")

"Zaydie, can't you stay awhile? I'm writing a story and need help with my Yiddish!"

"You're doing fine on your own. Just keep writing your stories!! Practice makes perfect. Now where can I take you for a brief visit before I bring you back home?"

"Anywhere is splendid if we're together! Please tell me about your life like you used to when I was a child! I love your stories!"

"*Vu zol ikh onheybn?*"

("Where should I start?")

As the train makes its way through the mountains, my beloved Zaydie takes me for a trip down memory lane.

The Little Things

When I was leaving the house, I saw one of our community's gardeners sitting under a tree eating lunch. I noticed he had no drink so I ran back into the house and grabbed a cold apple juice. I walked down our driveway and handed it to him. His English is limited, but no words were necessary. His eyes spoke volumes.

Sometimes it's the little things that can make a difference in someone's day. If a gesture of kindness or a loving word can uplift another human being, it is worth taking a moment to do it or say it.

For the past few years we were told to keep a "safe" distance from each other so we wouldn't catch germs. Our faces were covered so we couldn't share a smile. For many, the lack of human connection was difficult.

I think of this every day as I write my stories. Words have become our way of reaching out to each other. If we can touch each other lovingly with our words then all the viruses in the world won't keep us apart.

Like a garden that needs sunshine…

A lovely friendship will grow.

The Storyteller

Once in a while, someone will refer to me as the "Storyteller", and I always smile. Ever since I was a child, I have loved hearing people's life stories. I never considered it an annoyance to sit with my older relatives or even strangers while they reminisced about the old days. My imagination would be fueled by their stories.

Oftentimes someone will say, "My children and/or grandchildren aren't interested in my stories. They're too busy with electronic gadgets, and they're always glued to their phones."

Don't be discouraged from sharing your stories because decades from now when these young people reach the next chapter of their lives, something amazing will happen.

They will look in the mirror and see YOU staring back at them, perhaps those same eyes or that similar smile. They will lovingly remember you and the stories you shared at family gatherings. Even if their lives are totally different from yours, they will find themselves craving that connection to their roots.

They will find their way home.

Made in the USA
Monee, IL
23 May 2022